PRIMARY READERS
PRE-MOVERS

# Teamwork

**Brendan Dunne**
**Robin Newton**

Illustrator: Moreno Chiacchiera

This is Lara.

This is Maya.

Lara sits next to Maya at school, but are they friends? NOOOO!

Maya is very good at…

…maths. She can do really, really difficult sums!

…science. She can make really difficult potions!

…and computers. She always wins computer games!

Lara is very good at…

…climbing. She can climb up walls.

…gymnastics. She can do really, really difficult jumps.

…and running. She can run faster than anyone!

One day, the class visit the museum. They're getting on the bus. Maya pushes Lara. Then Lara pushes Maya. Oh no! They're fighting!

The children are looking at the diamond, but Lara and Maya are fighting **AGAIN!**

Oh no! Maya and Lara are fighting AGAIN!
The teacher is very angry. She tells the girls to go to reception NOW!

The girls go down to reception in the lift. | The girls make friends.

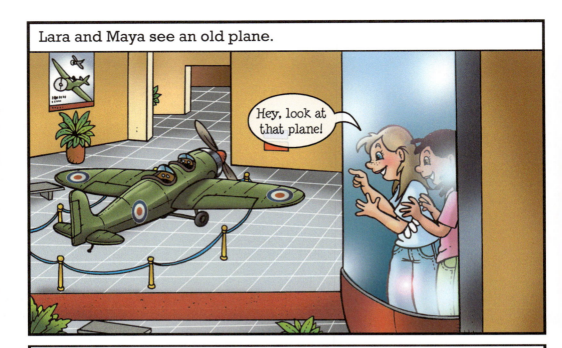

The class are going home. But where are Maya and Lara?

It's 6 o'clock and the museum is closed.
The girls are sleeping and nobody sees them.

It's night time and there's nobody in the museum. It's dark and quiet.

The girls find the control room, but they get a surprise.

11

Maya and Lara decide to save the diamond.

Lara's got the diamond now, but the burglars see her.

Lara is faster than the burglars. Run, Lara! Run!

Now, they're in the dinosaur room. Lara runs fast...

... but the burglars are VERY heavy.

Lara climbs up the wall. Don't fall Lara!

The police arrive. They see the burglars in the lift.

The police take the burglars away.

Lara and Maya are in the newspaper.
The police give them a special cup.

Lara and Maya are now VERY good friends.

# Picture Dictionary

23

# Picture Dictionary

| lift | lights | museum |
| --- | --- | --- |
| newspaper | plane | potion |
| sleep | sums | wall |